Seeing Things

By Allan Fowler

J
612.8
Fowler
C.1

10⁹⁵

Images supplied by VALAN Photos
and Jim Whitmer

Consultants:

Robert L. Hillerich, Ph.D., Bowling Green
State University, Bowling Green, Ohio

Mary Nalbandian, Director of Science,
Chicago Public Schools, Chicago, Illinois

Fay Robinson, Child Development Specialist

ℂℙ CHILDRENS PRESS®

CHICAGO

Series cover and interior design by Sara Shelton

Library of Congress Cataloging-in-Publication Data

Fowler, Allan.
    Seeing things / by Allan Fowler.
        p. cm.—(Rookie read-about science)
    Summary: Discusses the parts of the eye and how that organ works
to give us our view of the world.
    ISBN 0-516-04910-0
    1. Vision—Juvenile literature. [1. Eye. 2. Vision. 3. Senses
and sensation.] I. Title. II. Series.
QP475.7.F69   1991   90-22527
612.8'4—dc20   CIP
                                                                 AC

Your eyes show you so much!

They show you where
things are.

Did you ever play pin-the-tail-on-the-donkey?

With a blindfold on, you can't see anything. You keep pinning the tail in the wrong place.

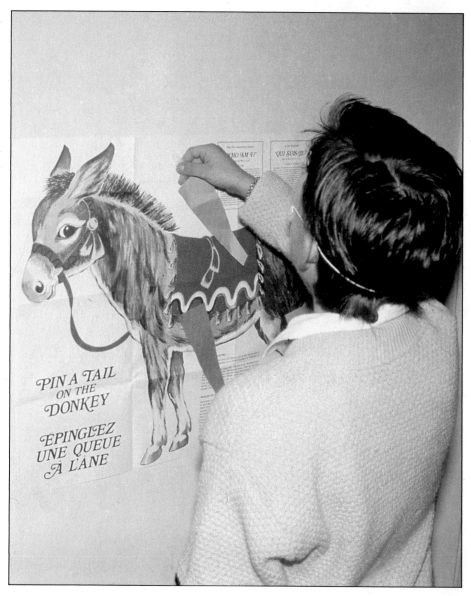

7

Your eyes show you if
something is far away
from you...

or close to you.

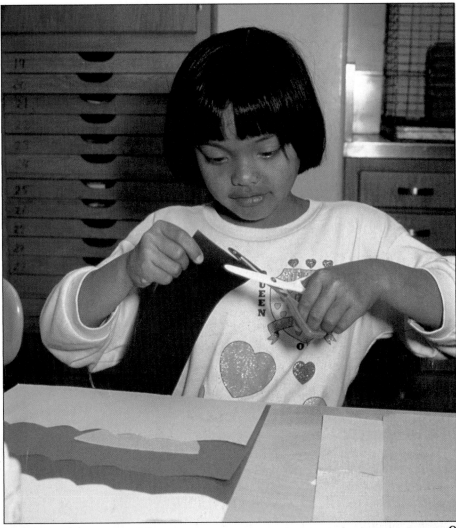

You use your eyes to see
where you're going...

so you don't bump into
things or trip over things.

Your eyes show you what shape things are...

and how big and what
color.

Your eyes show you who people are.

You know your
grandparents as soon as
you see them.

We call seeing the sense of sight.

With your five senses you
can see, hear, touch, smell,
and taste.

Here are some of the parts of your eye.

The iris is the colored part of your eye.

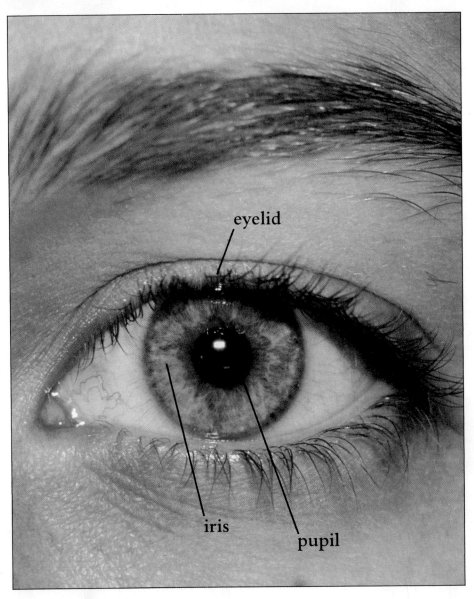

eyelid

iris

pupil

19

Most people have brown

or blue eyes...

green or gray eyes.

What color are your eyes?

Sometimes eyes need help.

Then people wear glasses.
Glasses help them see
better.

You should always take good care of your eyes.

To protect their eyes from the sun, people wear sunglasses or floppy hats.

Never look straight into
the sun. That could be
harmful.

Whenever you read, make sure there is plenty of light.

It's easier to read that way. And reading is one of the most important and most enjoyable things you can do with your eyes.

Words You Know

sense of sight

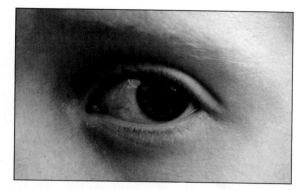

eye

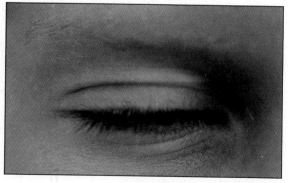

eyelid

iris

pupil

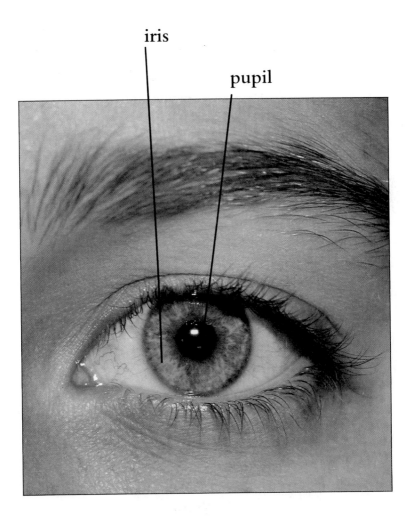

Index

About the Author

Allan Fowler is a free-lance writer with a background in advertising. Born in New York, he lives in Chicago now and enjoys traveling.

Photo Credits

Valan—© Robert C. Simpson, Cover, 21; © V. Wilkinson, 7, 19, 30 (2 photos), 31; © V. Whelan, 8, 11; © Fred Bruemmer, 12; © Stephen J. Krasemann, 13; © Kennon Cooke, 17, 20, 27

© Jim Whitmer—5, 9, 10, 15, 22, 25, 28

COVER: Jamie Simpson and cottontail